The Art of War for Photographers

The Mindset for a Successful Photography Business

By Bradley Lau

www.BradleyLau.com

© 2020 Bradley Lau

All rights reserved. No portion of this book may be reproduced in any form without permission from the publisher, except as permitted by U.S. copyright law. For permissions contact:

Brad@BradleyLau.com

Cover art by Saita Studio
Back cover photo by Dmytro Sobokar

Table of Contents

ABOUT THE ORIGINAL "ART OF WAR" 1

INTRODUCTION 2

CHAPTER 1: INITIAL PLANNING 5

CHAPTER 2: WAGING WAR 13

CHAPTER 3: ATTACK STRATEGY 16

CHAPTER 4: FORMATION AND POSITIONING 20

CHAPTER 5: POWER AND ENERGY 23

CHAPTER 6: WEAKNESS 26

CHAPTER 7: MANEVUERING 30

CHAPTER 8: FLEXIBILITY 33

CHAPTER 9: MARCHING ARMY 37

CHAPTER 10: TERRAIN 42

CHAPTER 11: SITUATIONS 47

CHAPTER 12: ATTACK BY FIRE 55

CHAPTER 13: THE USE OF SPIES 58

CONCLUSION 60

WORKBOOK SECTION 61

ABOUT THE AUTHOR 69

ABOUT THE ORIGINAL "ART OF WAR"

"The Art of War" was believed to be written by Sun Tzu, a Chinese military general, strategist and philosopher around 500 BC. As Sun Tzu was quite successful in his military battles, he wrote down his strategy on how to win wars and defeat his enemies.

This relatively simple book of military strategy has only 13 chapters, each chapter consisting of just a few pages in length. Is highly regarded by military experts and has been translated into many languages and used by military leaders world-wide. With many translations, comes many various versions, but naturally a common theme prevails.

INTRODUCTION

There has always been a correlation between war and business. In your business, you will always be battling or competing, and like all competitions, the goal is to win. In starting a photography business:

We win by making money and not losing it.

We win by having clients pick our services over the services of our competitors.

We win by having the best bid during the bidding process.

We win by having our clients completely satisfied.

We win by overcoming our own doubts and fears.

We win by thinking creatively.

We win by being organized.

We win by having a plan and executing it.

We win by having successful ad campaigns.

We win by overcoming office politics.

We lose by giving up.

We lose by not paying attention.

We lose because of sloppiness.

We lose because we do not adapt.

We lose because we do not anticipate.

We lose because of poor planning.

We lose because we manage our resources poorly.

We lose because we fail to follow up.

The list is endless.

We can take the strategies on how to win at war and apply them to our photography business. This does not mean you have to be a ruthless, blood thirsty, unethical photographer who sells their soul for the sake of a dollar. As a matter of fact, Sun Tzu said, "To win without fighting is best."

This book will shed light on basic principles that will help you to run a more successful photography business. You will be asked to think for yourself and apply these principles to your unique situation. While war involves battling your enemy, you may in fact have many "enemies".

Your enemy could be:

Yourself, your competitors, your subjects, present circumstances, pandemics, weather, traffic, distractions, decision makers, your equipment, your vendors, your employees, time, poor communication and the list goes on.

What other "enemies" can you add?

Also, while Sun Tzu refers to a leader and their army, in most instances, you will be a one-person army. You may not have any employees, but at times you still may have to collaborate with schedulers, art directors, assistants, subjects, makeup artists, retouchers, stylists, etc.

Finally, these principles and tactics have been simplified and I have used my own judgement on what to include and not include from the original texts. While I have photographed most genres, I currently shoot only headshots and my examples may reflect that. At times I've taken great liberty on how I interpret what Sun Tzu originally intended.

Sun Tzu's words are in **bold**.

CHAPTER 1: INITIAL PLANNING

The art of war is important to the country and is a matter of life and death.

As a photographer concentrating on creating your art, you can sometimes lose sight that in order to succeed financially, you must first treat your photography as a business. The success or life of your business, your career, your financial stability needs to be taken seriously as the death of your business will lead to financial loss.

Wake up every day ready to battle for your business and its success. Develop a business plan that will guide you to success. Start your day the way a disciplined warrior would.

What would be the best way for you to start your day?

A strong leader must have obedient and loyal followers.

Do you have repeat customers? Are your clients so loyal, they will come back to you over and over again and to only you? If another photographer approaches them, will they consider any offers given?

Develop a relationship with your clients and make it a joy for them to do business with you. Turn them into "fans" who will not switch teams for any reason.

The same applies to all of the people you work with. Maybe you have assistants, makeup artists, stylists, second shooters, retouchers, etc. that work with you. How loyal are they to you?

What are you doing to cultivate this loyalty? What can you do differently?

The Commander has wisdom, sincerity, benevolence, courage and strictness.

We all know of the challenges that each new shoot brings. Problem solving abilities come from experience and with this experience you gain wisdom. Stretch yourself by giving yourself new projects to shoot that are a bit out of your comfort zone. Think of one new shoot you can do next week that may be a bit different that will stretch you a bit.

Be honest and fair in all of your business dealings. Do you have any guarantees? What is the procedure for dissatisfied clients?

Kindness goes a long way for all of those that you work with. Give genuine compliments, especially if you photograph people. Do the people that work with you consider you a delight to work with or a pain in the neck?

Be willing to take risks. Have the courage to try new things, both from a business standpoint as well as a creative one. Maybe try a new ad campaign or a new lighting setup that the client may or may not like.

Be strict with your professionalism. Never be late yourself and do not tolerate it with any of those you work with. Let clients know lateness can turn into a domino effect your shooting schedule for the rest of the day. Request that your clients are to be ready a set number of minutes before the shoot. You need to be able to fire those who are habitually late. Be strict with your attention to detail. Never allow "good enough" to be a part of you or your business.

What do you need to work on?

A winning army will have harmony between Commander and army.

There should be respect between you and your clients and those you work with. Being difficult and having friction points presents opportunity for failure. Can you think of any friction points that exist with you or your business?

Location is important.

You should know the terrain your battle will be on. As a photographer, do you scout out new locations when you have new shoots? Or do you just show up and learn as you go? Take the time to learn about all of the areas of your shooting location for potential shooting ideas. You should also know about traffic and potential delays the terrain might produce. How does the sun look at different times of the day for a particular location and how will it affect your shoot?

If you have your own studio where clients come to you, how easy is it for them to get to you? Is it close to major highways or public transportation? Is there adequate parking? Is it easy to find? Is it warm and inviting?

If you have your own studio location, what can you do to improve it?

Discipline must be enforced along the chain of command.

The people that you work with must know that there are consequences when things go wrong and that they must take responsibility for their actions. If you are always easy, you will be considered a pushover and people will take advantage of you. Here's an extreme Sun Tzu example to illustrate the point. (Please don't be this harsh)

Ssu-ma Ch'ien gives the following biography of Sun Tzu:
Sun Tzu Wu was a native of the Ch'i State. His Art of War brought him to the notice of Ho Lu, King of Wu. Ho Lu said to him:

"I have carefully perused your 13 chapters. May I submit your theory of managing soldiers to a slight test?"

Sun Tzu replied: "You may."

Ho Lu asked: "May the test be applied to women?"

The answer was again in the affirmative, so arrangements were made to bring 180 ladies out of the Palace. Sun Tzu divided them into two companies and placed one of the King's favorite concubines at the head of each. He then bade them all take spears in their hands, and addressed them thus: "I presume you know the difference between front and back, right hand and left hand?"

The girls replied: Yes.

Sun Tzu went on: "When I say, "Eyes front," you must look straight ahead. When I say, "Left turn," you must face towards your left hand. When I say, "Right turn," you must face towards your right hand. When I say, "About turn," you must face right round towards your back."

Again, the girls assented. The words of command having been thus explained, he set up the halberds and battle-axes in order to begin the drill. Then, to the sound of drums, he gave the order "Right turn." But the girls only burst out laughing. Sun Tzu said: "If words of command are not clear and distinct, if orders are not thoroughly understood, then the general is to blame."

So, he started drilling them again, and this time gave the order "Left turn," whereupon the girls once more burst into fits of laughter.

Sun Tzu: "If words of command are not clear and distinct, if orders are not thoroughly understood, the general is to blame. But if his orders are clear, and the soldiers nevertheless disobey, then it is the fault of their officers."

So, saying, he ordered the leaders of the two companies to be beheaded. Now the king of Wu was watching the scene from the top of a raised pavilion; and when he saw that his favorite concubines were about to be executed, he was greatly alarmed and hurriedly sent down the following message: "We are now quite satisfied as to our general's ability to handle troops. If we are bereft of these two concubines, our meat and drink will lose their savor. It is our wish that they shall not be beheaded."

Sun Tzu replied: "Having once received His Majesty's commission to be the general of his forces, there are certain commands of His Majesty which, acting in that capacity, I am unable to accept."

Accordingly, he had the two leaders beheaded, and straightway installed the pair next in order as leaders in their place. When this had been done, the drum was sounded for the drill once more; and the girls went through all the evolutions, turning to the right or to the left, marching ahead or wheeling back, kneeling or standing, with perfect accuracy and precision, not venturing to utter a sound.

Then Sun Tzu sent a messenger to the King saying: "Your soldiers, Sire, are now properly drilled and disciplined, and ready for your majesty's inspection. They can be put to any use that their sovereign may desire; bid them go through fire and water, and they will not disobey."

But the King replied: "Let our general cease drilling and return to camp. As for us, we have no wish to come down and inspect the troops."

Thereupon Sun Tzu said: "The King is only fond of words and cannot translate them into deeds."

After that, Ho Lu saw that Sun Tzu was one who knew how to handle an army, and finally appointed him general. In the west, he defeated the Ch'u State and forced his way into Ying, the capital; to the north he put fear into the States of Ch'i and Chi and spread his fame abroad amongst the feudal princes. And Sun Tzu shared in the might of the King.

Please don't chop anyone's head off.

Winners must be morally and physically strong.

Morally, do the right thing when it comes to your business and how you treat the people you come in contact with. Don't overbill even if you think you can get away with it. Don't sneak in extra charges and make sure your clients are always aware of your pricing details.

If you have failed to deliver in anyway, make sure you fix it. That may mean reshooting at your own expense.

Physically, make sure you are strong enough to have the energy to do your job well. Are you fit and in shape? Or are you tired and a bit sluggish? I remember having to quit shooting weddings many years ago because I was so beat up after shooting a weekend of weddings. I found it difficult to walk on Mondays and was physically shot and basically useless the day after. Whatever your age, work at being physically fit for both you and your clients. You will not only feel better, perform better, you will also look commanding. Do your clients see you as a sloppy mess or fit and energetic?

Winners must be well trained.

It goes without saying you must be knowledgeable. While you don't need formal training, you must educate yourself. You must know your gear inside and out. Pull out your camera manual and read it again. You must know various lighting techniques to overcome the problems that you may encounter. What areas of photography are you standoffish about? Maybe you only shoot natural light and are afraid to use flash. Challenge yourself to learn new things. What new technique do you wish to learn that will help you with your business? What online course or workshop can you take that you can benefit from?

Winners must have a willingness to be flexible.

Don't be rigid doing the same things over and over again. Challenge yourself to try new things. When a shoot isn't going right, methodically look for a different solution. If clients change appointment times, be willing to be somewhat flexible. If a client wants to try something that you know won't work, be willing to try and accommodate them.

All warfare is based on deception.

What tricks do you use in your business? By this I mean, what do you do to make it look easy? Keep in mind the previous points about the importance of sincerity and benevolence. We don't advocate deceptive sales or business practices or immoral behavior. Distraction is also a form of deception. Sometimes we need to distract our clients, especially if they are uncomfortable people, children or pets. It can be as simple as a question like what's your favorite food, a loud noise or whistle, or a fun, outrageous comment.

Cause division among your enemy including bribery.

Maybe there's a client you have wanted for a long time. Maybe sending a "bribe" of a gift basket or gift certificate, may help you land the business. The Law of Reciprocity states that if I give you something, you are more inclined to give me something back. This sales tactic works and does not have to be sleazy. Maybe you give a free session in hopes of getting additional sales. What can you do to give in order to get?

Don't talk about your plans right before battle.

While this refers to spies learning about our plans, we can read this to mean that talk is cheap. Actions speak louder than words. What have you been talking about regarding your business that you have wanted to do for a while, but keep putting off?

Taking the opposite view, when dealing with clients on a shoot, it is good to tell them your plans in great detail, so they know exactly what to expect. It will make them feel more comfortable.

Generals who plan ahead win. Those who don't will lose.

This is the most important lesson of this chapter. Winging it doesn't work. Every battle has a plan. Every sports team has a coach mapping out play-by-play as the game progresses. Actors rehearse their lines over and over. By planning you will be more prepared.

What is the plan for your business? What are your monthly profit goals? What will you have to do in order to achieve them?

CHAPTER 2: WAGING WAR

War costs a thousand ounces of silver per day for an army of 100,000 men.

A photography business needs capital to start and function properly. Your business needs to be profitable. You are doing yourself a disservice if you only scrape by as a photographer. Make sure your rates are high enough and that you have a number of upsells to offer your clients, so you can make a nice living for yourself. Do not be a low-end provider competing only on price. You will work too hard for too little.

Read the above paragraph one hundred more times.

In battle, if victory takes a long time, the weapons will grow dull and enthusiasm will be damped.

Be as efficient as possible during your shoots. Time is money. Don't waste your time or your clients time. Be quick and decisive. If you are shooting people, long shoots will tire them out and the results will not be as good.

I remember once reading about a famous person that was in their backyard and a photographer was coming to their house to take their picture for the cover of a magazine. The photographer arrived, snapped the shutter one time and started to walk away. The famous person asked, "Why did you only take one photo?" The photographer confidently responded, "because only one photo is needed for the cover and I nailed it." This was pre digital. What confidence this photographer must have had in themselves! (If anyone knows the actual story, let me know.)

If the campaign is quick, the resources of the State will not be equal to the strain.

Make sure your efforts are worthwhile. Beginners are often asked to do a lot of free work. Be careful of what projects you choose.

Now, when your weapons are dulled, your enthusiasm damped, your strength exhausted and your treasure spent, other chieftains will spring up to take advantage of your extremity. Then no man, however wise, will be able to avert the consequences that must ensue.

If you overwork yourself, spread yourself too thin, you may find other competitors coming to take your business. Don't let the enemy of exhaustion creep in.

Bring war material with you from home, but forage on the enemy. Thus, the army will have food enough for its needs.

If you have to travel far for a shoot, consider renting gear instead of bringing all of your own. Make sure you bring everything with you that you will need for a successful shoot.

With this loss of substance and exhaustion of strength, the homes of the people will be stripped bare, and 3/10's of their income will be dissipated.

As a photographer, take your job and business seriously. Your family income and resources should not be wasted. When you get bored, don't just buy new equipment for the sake of it, hoping some magical will come of it. Be resourceful and work with what you have.

Now in order to kill the enemy, our men must be roused to anger; that there may be advantage from defeating the enemy, they must have their rewards.

Be passionate about your work and charge enough to make it worth your while.

Captured soldiers should be kindly treated and kept.

Treat your competitors well. In fact, get to know them. Have lunch with them. You will find it may become profitable for you both, to refer business that you may not want or be able to take, to each other.

In war, then, let your great object be victory, not lengthy campaigns.

Be efficient with your time. I remember spending so much time retouching my headshot images. I could easily spend an hour on an image. I would zoom in so much and fix things that no one saw with the naked eye. What are you spending too much time on?

CHAPTER 3: ATTACK STRATEGY

In the practical art of war, the best thing of all is to take the enemy's country whole and intact; to shatter and destroy it is not so good.

Well you certainly don't want to shatter and destroy your equipment. Always safely secure lights and light stands. Use your camera strap when possible. Add a UV filter to protect your lenses. Use the lens hood even indoors. If you drop the camera, the lens hood may take most of the impact and will be cheaper to replace than the lens.

Hence to fight and conquer in all your battles is not supreme excellence; supreme excellence consists in breaking the enemy's resistance without fighting.

Maybe you get resistance to your prices. How can you create enough value that you will not have to battle with your customer to justify your prices?

What can you do to eliminate any resistance from clients hiring you?

The general, unable to control his irritation, will launch his men to the assault like swarming ants.

Impatience in general, is never any good. If you find yourself getting irritated, this may affect how the subject feels and the final outcome of the phots may lack the quality they should have. Realize humans aren't perfect and make mistakes. Try and always deliver a great experience for your clients and with those you work with. This happens to me sometimes when clients are late. Breathe!

Therefore, the skillful leader subdues the enemy's troops without any fighting; he captures their cities without laying siege to them; he overthrows their kingdom without lengthy operations in the field.

What can you do to smooth out the interactions that you have with your clients and those you work with? Win them over before your shoot even starts and before they see any photos.

There are three ways in which a ruler can bring misfortune upon his army:

By commanding the army to advance or to retreat, being ignorant of the fact that it cannot obey. This is called hobbling the army.

Don't ask people to do things they can't do. Sometimes people can't pose in the way I want them to due to their physical limitations.

By attempting to govern an army in the same way as he administers a kingdom, being ignorant of the conditions which obtain in an army. This causes restlessness in the soldier's minds.

Make sure you are ready to go when your clients are there. Don't let them get restless because you are not prepared.

By employing the officers of his army without discrimination, through ignorance of the military principle of adaptation to circumstances. This shakes the confidence of the soldiers.

Be a good leader and try and separate yourself from your business. Don't do things personally to the detriment of your business. Be willing to say no to jobs that you are not qualified to do. Don't put yourself into hot water. Hire the right people for the job, especially jobs you are not suited for. Basically, do the things you should do, even if you don't "feel" like it.

Thus, we may know that there are five essentials for victory:

He will win who knows when to fight and when not to fight.

Know when do be flexible with those you deal with. Hard engagement may not always be the best solution.

He will win who knows how to handle both superior and inferior forces.

Learn how to shoot the big jobs and the little jobs. You should feel comfortable interacting with the low-level employees as well as CEO's.

He will win whose army is animated by the same spirit throughout all its ranks.

Your shooting environment should be a fun place to be in for all involved. Keep the energy high. Don't play favorites.

He will win who prepared himself, waits to take the enemy unprepared.

It's pretty obvious that you need to be prepared. Check all your gear, shoot lists, schedules, and have a full understanding of what you are to accomplish. Acting confident will make your clients feel better.

Never tryout new equipment that you haven't used before on a paying client. Even new, out of the box equipment sometimes malfunctions.

He will win who has military capacity and is not interfered with by the sovereign.

You're the boss. Don't let others call the shots. Sometimes clients fight with me when I pose them. They go off on their own and I know it looks bad. While I give them some slack and let them do their thing, I'll quickly reign them in and ask them to now try my way. This happens a lot with people who used to model. They go into "model mode" which looks bad for a corporate headshot.

If you know the enemy and know yourself, you need not fear the result of a hundred battles. If you know yourself but not the enemy, for every victory gained you will also suffer a defeat. If you know neither the enemy nor yourself, you will succumb in every battle.

Know your stuff, plain and simple. Show up as a pro, ready to go. Practice constantly.

CHAPTER 4: FORMATION AND POSITIONING

The good fighters of old first put themselves beyond the possibility of defeat and then waited for an opportunity of defeating the enemy.

Don't put yourself or your business in challenging positions where you can fail. Set yourself up for success. You may need to shoot multiple genres. You may need to add video. Having multiple streams of income may be necessary for your business.

Thus, the good fighter is able to secure himself against defeat.

Take precautions and be careful. What risks have you taken recently that have backfired? Have you showed up to a wedding with only one camera?

Security against defeat implies defensive tactics; ability to defeat the enemy means taking the offensive.

Always take the initiative. Being shy or bashful will never get you anywhere in life. Be confident. If you don't have it, fake it until you do.

The general who is skilled in defense hides in the most secret recesses of the earth.

Stealth is sometimes necessary. I used to have problems going into office buildings in Manhattan with tight security. They would make a big deal about all the equipment I had.

I greatly reduced every bit of equipment so I could roll in with one carry-on bag filled to the brim without raising any suspicion. This eliminated having to use freight elevators which are slower and the added insurance liability insurance. I have tons of insurance, but it is always a pain in the neck to issue the paperwork that comes with it.

He who is skilled in attack flashes forth from the topmost heights of heaven.

Be fast. Know your gear and don't fuss with your equipment. Get your shots quickly. Know exactly how and where to position your lighting.

What the ancients called a clever fighter is one who not only wins but excels in winning with ease.

Make it look easy through experience, practice, a plan, and the ability to anticipate issues before they arise. Put your 10,000 hours in as quickly as you can to become an expert.

He wins his battles by making no mistakes.

Small mistakes happen for sure; I can certainly count many I make every week. Work at not repeating the same mistakes.

Hence the skillful fighter puts himself into a position which makes defeat impossible and does not miss the moment for defeating the enemy.

This certainly holds true for event photography. Be ready and prepared not to miss the exact moment to capture a great photo. Stop staring at the back of your LCD screen all the time, missing opportunities.

Thus, it is that in war the victorious strategist only seeks battle after the victory has been won, whereas he who is destined to defeat first fights and afterwards looks for victory.

"If you fail to plan, you plan to fail." – Benjamin Franklin

CHAPTER 5: POWER AND ENERGY

The control of a large force is the same principle as the control of a few men: it is merely a question of dividing up their numbers.

This reminds me of the saying, "How do you eat an elephant? – One bite at a time."

Break any large task into smaller, manageable tasks and you will not be overwhelmed. Do you have any large projects that you have been avoiding? Figure out how to break them down into the smallest of steps and start checking each item off the list.

In all fighting, the direct method may be used for joining battle, but indirect methods will be needed in order to secure victory.

You need to attack the enemy from the rear and sides and not just head on.

Think about adding additional lights when shooting. It's the rim lights, hair lights and background lights that often make an image better and don't just concentrate on just a main key light illuminating the front object. What else can you do to indirectly improve your business? Even a trip to a museum to get inspired can help.

There are not more than five musical notes, yet the combinations of these five give rise to more melodies than can ever be heard.

There are not more than five primary colors (blue, yellow, red, white, and black), yet in combination they produce more hues than can ever been seen. There are not more than five cardinal tastes (sour, acrid, salt, sweet, bitter), yet combinations of them yield more flavors than can ever be tasted.

Consider complexity when you can. Add extra layers to your shoots. Foreground, midground, background. Add more lights to highlight the different layers. Consider different wardrobes, scenery, and backgrounds. Try using gels.

If you are shooting plain background headshots, consider adding some environmental shots. If you are shooting real estate, shoot the outside of the house during daylight hours as well as the night.

The quality of decision is like the well-timed swoop of a falcon which enables it to strike and destroy its victim.

Good timing is everything so be patient and wait for the exact right moment to take action. Don't just be a "spray and pray" photographer. Be deliberate when you press the shutter release.

Make the decisions for your business that will be beneficial in the long run. Cultivate relationships that will help your business in the long run.

The clever combatant looks to the effect of combined energy, and does not require too much from individuals, hence his ability to pick out the right men and utilize combined energy.

Consider partnerships and working with others. Get a team to help you with your business. Do not be afraid to outsource things such as retouching. Learn to let go. Others may not do as good a job as you, but it may still be quite acceptable to you and your clients. And others may in fact to a better job than you.

I always hated the idea of farming out my retouching. Anytime I tried, I was never happy with the results. After continuous searching, I finally found someone I like and the amount of time savings I now have is amazing. It's the best thing I've ever done. BUILD A TEAM!!

CHAPTER 6: WEAKNESS

Whoever is first in the field and awaits the coming of the enemy, will be fresh for the fight; whoever is second in the field and has to hasten to battle will arrive exhausted.

Don't show up late to any photoshoot or appointment so you don't appear rushed or frazzled. It's a good habit to develop to always be early so you can be in the best mental state possible.

Therefore, the clever combatant imposes his will on the enemy, but does not allow the enemy's will to be imposed on him.

Be a strong force in your field and circle of competitors. Have the power of your convictions and stick to what you believe in. Let your clients know they hired you because you are the expert. I have my clients pick their own headshot photo for retouching. If they pick the "wrong" one, I'll let them know. I'm not shy about it. "This isn't as good as this one because of x, y, and z."

Appear at points which the enemy must hasten to defend; march swiftly to places where you are not expected.

Be lean and agile. Have the ability to move and change your business at will. Always be willing to adapt. Remember Kodak? They didn't adapt to digital. But in 2020 they are adapting to produce pharmaceutical ingredients.

An army may march great distances without distress, if it marches through country where the enemy is not.

Market in areas where there is little competition. Is there anywhere else, relatively close by, where you can market your business?

Hence that general is skillful in attack whose opponent does not know what to defend; and he is skillful in defense whose opponent does not know what to attack.

Don't let your competitors outsmart you. Are you aware of who they are, what they are offering, and what clients they have?

You may advance and be absolutely irresistible, if you make for the enemy's weak points; you may retire and be safe from pursuit if your movements are more rapid than those of the enemy.

Always be ahead of your competition. Try and be the leader of your industry. What are you doing to innovate? Look at other industries and see how they innovate. Can you use any of their ideas for your business? What can you offer your clients that the competition isn't offering?

Carefully compare the opposing army with your own, so that you may know where strength is superabundant and where it is deficient.

Understand who your competitors are and what they are offering. Know where you are weak and work on strengthening those areas.

In making tactical dispositions, the highest pitch you can attain is to conceal them; conceal your dispositions, and you will be safe from the prying of the subtlest spies, from the machinations of the wisest brains.

This reminds me of the gambling phrase, "play your cards close to the vest." Maybe consider not putting all of your information on your website. Some argue this point, especially when it comes to pricing. I personally put my pricing on my site. The principle is not to display everything.

Also, as a beginner, don't make the mistake of showing every photo you have on your website portfolio. Cull your images and only show your best work. It's better to show only 3 great images instead of 15 mediocre ones.

How victory may be produced for them out of the enemy's own tactics—that is what the multitude cannot comprehend.

What is your competitor offering or not offering that may be viewed as a disadvantage to them? Maybe they only do studio work. If so, maybe consider going to your clients' location.

All men can see the tactics whereby I conquer, but what none can see is the strategy out of which victory is evolved.

People might see your success and think it's easy. They don't see all of the work, planning, effort and skill that goes into it.

Do not repeat the tactics which have gained you one victory, but let your methods be regulated by the infinite variety of circumstances.

Don't fall into a rut and do the same things over and over again. Be creative and explore other options. This may include how you light, how you market and perhaps what you shoot. If you were to add an additional segment to your business, what would it be? (video, weddings, products, real estate, etc.)

Just as water retains no constant shape, so in warfare there are no constant conditions.

You have to be adaptable. Don't be stubborn. See the writing on the wall if it comes and learn to make changes easily and swiftly. Remember Kodak!

He who can modify his tactics in relation to his opponent and thereby succeed in winning, may be called a heaven-born captain.

You must always be willing to adapt and adjust. Are you a heaven-born photographer? Also, be willing to adjust to your client's needs.

CHAPTER 7: MANEVUERING

Having collected an army and concentrated his forces, he must blend and harmonize the different elements thereof before pitching his camp.

Before starting a shoot, there should be harmony among everyone involved, so confidence will be felt by all parties involved.

You should also have all your equipment ready to go, out and available. You shouldn't be making adjustments or setting up while your client is in front of you. This is like the cooking equivalent to the French phrase "mise en place" – everything in its place. This means everything you need to cook a meal is already prepped and readily available. Everything necessary for your shoot should be neatly laid out.

We may take it then that an army without its baggage-train is lost; without provisions it is lost; without bases of supply it is lost.

Make sure you have the proper gear for the job you are doing. Especially if you go onsite to clients, make sure you have everything you could possibly need.

We are not fit to lead an army on the march unless we are familiar with the face of the country—its mountains and forests, its pitfalls and precipices, its marshes and swamps.

Know the lay of the land. Scope out shooting locations prior to shooting if you are not familiar with the location.

We shall be unable to turn natural advantage to account unless we make use of local guides.

Locals may have some ideas for you to help you improve your shoots. Always ask if you are on location, if there are any good spots they could recommend for you to shoot in besides the obvious ones.

In war, practice dissimulation, and you will succeed.

Deception is a huge part of Sun Tzu's beliefs. Make everything look easy and be well prepared. Don't let your clients know if you are having a hard time with something.

Let your rapidity be that of the wind, your compactness that of the forest.

The wind is fast and leaves no trace. Be tightly packed and compact. It makes movement easier. Pack light. I once saw a wedding photographer show up to a wedding with a ton of gear attached all over her body while holding a large off camera ring light. The wedding was on a party bus where all of the out of town guests could view the ceremony and all of the sights of Manhattan after it. There was just no room on this crowded bus, and I witnessed this photographer struggle in such a confined space with all of her gear.

Do your recon and go lean and mean when you have to.

Let your plans be dark and impenetrable as night, and when you move, fall like a thunderbolt.

Be swift and deliberate. Move with a purpose. Have a perfect plan.

When you plunder a countryside, let the spoil be divided amongst your men; when you capture new territory, cut it up into allotments for the benefit of the soldiery.

If you have a team, share the wealth. Be generous with those that help you and have ready some tip money for anyone you encounter that is a great help to you when deemed necessary. This certainly will not always be the case but be prepared. Just like you should always have business cards on you, you should also have a few bills handy. In this day and age, it's so easy to walk around with zero cash.

If you are lucky enough to have someone that refers you business, make sure you repay them in some way. Thank yous are not enough.

Ponder and deliberate before you make a move.

As my momma always said, "think before you act."

CHAPTER 8: FLEXIBILITY

In hemmed-in situations, you must resort to stratagem. In desperate position, you must fight.

Your strategy and aggressiveness will help you to win. Make sure you work at developing both. How hard are you working to find new clients? Aggressiveness can simply be how hard you work, so don't use the excuse you are not aggressive by nature. Be aggressive with all aspects of your business. How hard did you fight for your business today?

There are roads which must not be followed, armies which must be not attacked, towns which must not be besieged, positions which must not be contested, commands of the sovereign which must not be obeyed.

We all have different paths. When I first started as a photographer, I called myself a whore. "Pay me and I'll shoot it" was my mantra. I shot actor headshots, weddings, families, babies, pets, corporate headshots, products, jewelry, furniture, real estate, bar mitzvahs, birthday parties, corporate events, photobooth, model portfolios, etc. etc.

But I learned as time went on that I only wanted to shoot one thing, corporate headshots. I cut ties to all of those genres, stopped advertising in those areas, and removed all images that weren't headshots. For me it was the best decision I made. You don't need to go down every path. You don't need to say yes to every job request. Pick and choose what is right for you as best as you can.

Learn to trust your gut. If a job or client doesn't seem right for you, turn them down. This may hurt financially, but sometimes it's the best thing you can do for your sanity.

The general who thoroughly understands the advantages that accompany variation of tactics knows how to handle his troops. The general who does not understand these, may be well acquainted with the configuration of the country, yet he will not be able to turn his knowledge to practical account.

Take advantage of the natural surroundings and use them to your benefit. In the same way, take advantage of your natural talents and use them to your advantage. If you have great people skills and you stay stuck in a studio shooting only products, you may wish to consider shooting people. And certainly, the opposite applies.

Add variation to all of your shoots. At the end of my shoots if time permits, I always try and experiment and stray from the normal tried and true way of shooting. These experimental shots may be an opportunity for you to sell more images.

So, the student of war who is unversed in the art of war of varying his plans, will fail to make the best use of his men. If, on the other hand, in the midst of difficulties we are always ready to seize an advantage, we may extricate ourselves from misfortune.

Plans change. Be flexible. When things change, always focus on solutions, not the problem. Look for opportunities as they arise and jump on them if you can. Keep up with your local news to learn about opportunities that may present themselves.

There are five dangerous faults which may affect a general:

Recklessness, which leads to destruction;

Don't be reckless with your camera gear. Things fall and drop and break. Keep your gear secure! If you pass off your camera to have them see the LCD, make sure they use the strap or better yet, just hold it for them.

cowardice, which leads to capture;

Fess up to your mistakes when you make them and don't hide from your clients if you screw up. Take the chances that you should take. Don't be meek.

a hasty temper, which can be provoked by insults;

You must always be in control of your mood. Clients and coworkers should never see you get frustrated. Keep it to yourself when things aren't going well. So many times, I've had software issues that effected my tethered shooting. On occasion, I bitched how much I hated the software. I know my clients don't care. Fix things quietly. It was a mistake to verbalize my frustration.

a delicacy of honor which is sensitive to shame;

Don't be thin skinned. If you ever ask for critiques or if clients aren't happy, don't take is so personally that you get bent out of shape over it. Accept constructive criticism and ask for it from more experienced peers.

over-caring for his men, which exposes him to worry and trouble.

Don't obsess and worry over certain situations. Most of the time things work out for the best and we worry for no reason.

CHAPTER 9: MARCHING ARMY

We come now to the question of encamping the army and observing signs of the enemy. Camp in high places. Do not climb heights in order to fight. So much for mountain warfare. After crossing a river, you should get far away from it.

Here we can consider the importance of "positioning". How you position your business is vitally important. Will you be the high end, custom boutique or will you be the "Walmart" of your industry?

If you are anxious to fight, you should not go to meet the invader near a river which he has to cross.

Rivers aside, what makes you anxious? How can you prepare better to eliminate your anxiety?

Moor your craft higher up than the enemy and facing the sun.

When shooting outdoors, always consider the position of the sun and how it will affect your shoot. When shooting portraits, it's nice to have the setting sun behind your subjects making for a great hair light.

All armies prefer high ground to low and sunny places to dark.

Think about your height when shooting. If you are shooting children or pets, get to their level. When shooting headshots, shoot them so they look like the exact same height as you. To give someone a feeling of power or height, shoot lower, looking up at them. If glare appears in your subjects' glasses, raise the height of your lights and have the subject lower their gaze.

When in consequence of heavy rains up-country, a river which you wish to cross is swollen and flecked with foam, you must wait until it subsides.

If you have to shoot outside when it is raining, make sure your gear is waterproof and that your constantly check to make sure there are no water marks on your lens. Hire an assistant to hold a large umbrella for you. They also make rain covers for gear you may want to have in your bag.

While not the norm, you may encounter this if you are shooting a wedding and you can't change the date.

If in the neighborhood of your camp there should be any hilly country, ponds surrounded by aquatic grass, hollow basins filled with reeds, or woods with thick undergrowth, they must be carefully routed out and searched; for these are places where men in ambush or insidious spies are likely to be lurking.

There may be bad people around waiting to steal your equipment. I've read stories of photographers getting their gear stolen from their cars. This also happens on location. Don't tempt people with an open bag of lenses. This has happened to wedding photographers who put down their gear without securing it.

When the enemy is close at hand and remains quiet, he is relying on the natural strength of his position. When he keeps aloof and tries to provoke a battle, he is anxious for the other side to advance.

Learn how to read your clients and act accordingly. I personally have a very fun, carefree, easygoing attitude and persona when I am photographing my headshot clients, even with top CEO's. But some people, regardless of title don't want the lighthearted atmosphere.

I also, while a "touchy" subject, (pun intended), touch my clients to fix collars, ties, hair, jewelry, with permission of course. For me it's necessary, just as a hairdresser has to touch their client. I am intuitive enough to know the very few who say OK but find it uncomfortable. I immediately stop. I do find that 99% thank me for being so detail oriented.

The rising of birds in their flight is the sign of an ambuscade. When there is dust rising in a high column, it is the sign of chariots advancing; when the dust is low, but spread over a wide area, it betokens the approach of infantry.

Learn to read the signs that your clients are giving off. Learn to read the signs of your industry and keep up with any changes that are happening. Befriend other photographers in and out of your genre.

Peace proposals unaccompanied by a sworn covenant indicate a plot.

Make sure you get everything in writing, so you and your client know exactly what to expect, especially on larger jobs. In addition to contracts, make sure all your paperwork is in order including model releases, contracts, proposals, and tax documents.

When an army feeds its horses with grain and kills its cattle for food, (In the ordinary course of things, the men would be fed on grain and the horses

chiefly on grass) and when the men do not hang their cooking-pots over the camp-fires, showing that they will not return to their tents, you may know that they are determined to fight to the death.

Are you aware of any of your strong competitors gearing up to take the market by storm and stop at nothing to be a success? Are there any freight trains coming your way that you don't know about? This determined attitude should be cultivated by you for your own business.

When envoys are sent with compliments in their mouths, it is a sign that the enemy wishes for a truce.

As stated earlier, teaming up with your competitors may be a good idea. I'm sure you have had jobs you had to say no to. They may have them as well. Why not share with each other and help each other out so you both benefit?

He who exercises no forethought but makes light of his opponents is sure to be captured by them.

Don't take your competition lightly. They may be out to take your livelihood, either on purpose or just by default because they are better than you. As Andy Grove, the CEO of Intel said, "only the paranoid survive."

Therefore, soldiers must be treated in the first instance with humanity but kept under control by means of iron discipline. This is a certain road to victory.

While you can direct this passage to your employees if you have any, you can also direct this towards yourself. Be kind to yourself as you should always be your best cheerleader.

And if you can lead a disciplined life and do the hard things you know you should do, you will have much more success and victory.

CHAPTER 10: TERRAIN

We may distinguish six kinds of terrain, to wit: (1) Accessible ground; (2) entangling ground; (3) temporizing ground i.e. ground which allows you to delay (4) narrow passes; (5) precipitous heights; (6) positions at a great distance from the enemy. Ground which can be freely traversed by both sides is called accessible.

When picking a studio location, make sure it is easy to get to by your clients with ample parking and transportation. A home location may also be considered if you can make it feel like a studio where your clients will feel comfortable. Make sure that it is big enough so it's easy to move around and navigate without knocking into light stands and your other equipment. Make sure people feel safe at your location.

With regard to ground of this nature, be before the enemy in occupying the raised and sunny spots, and carefully guard your line of supplies.

Always be the first one to arrive and make sure your equipment is looked after.

From a position of this sort, if the enemy is unprepared, you may sally forth and defeat him. But if the enemy is prepared for your coming, and you fail to defeat him, then, return being impossible, disaster will ensue.

Be prepared, for those that aren't, will lose. Always have a game plan before you start a shoot. Make sure you have a complete game plan and vision for your business.

When the position is such that neither side will gain by making the first move, it is called temporizing ground. (Both sides are stuck.)

Try and recognize quickly when you are stuck or in a rut. Create some projects that are different for you. Create new marketing plans that you normally wouldn't do. Photography is such a great business where your creativity can help you to explore new possibilities.

If you are situated at a great distance from the enemy, and the strength of the two armies is equal, it is not easy to provoke a battle, and fighting will be to your disadvantage.

Long commutes are tiring for you and your clients. Don't make them travel far to you and do your best to have your business studio as close to you as possible.

Other conditions being equal, if one force is hurled against another ten times its size, the result will be the flight of the former.

What can you do to dominate your market so that all of your competitors won't stand a chance? Start to become obsessed with growing your business. Make sure you keep the right accounting records so you can see how good or bad you are doing.

When the officers are too strong and the common soldiers too weak, the result is collapse.

If you have employees, don't work them to death. And if you are a type A workaholic, don't push yourself to the point of collapse. It's good to be driven but maintain a healthy balance of work and play. When I have full day shoots, I make sure to schedule in a 15-minute mid-morning break, a 30-minute lunch break and another 15-minute afternoon break. I leave the shooting area during these times to recharge.

When the higher officers are angry and insubordinate, and on meeting the enemy give battle on their own account from a feeling of resentment, before the commander-in-chief can tell whether or not he is in a position to fight, the result is ruin.

Don't work angry for whatever reason. Control you temper if you have one. Otherwise, it will only lead to ruin. Anger isn't conducive for creativity.

When the general is weak and without authority; when his orders are not clear and distinct; when there are no fixed duties assigned to officers and men, and the ranks are formed in a slovenly haphazard manner, the result is utter disorganization.

If you photograph people, make sure you know how to communicate with them, so they understand how you want them to pose. With all your clients, make your email communications clear and concise. But don't respond with simple one-word responses. Use their names and make your responses feel personalized.

Make sure you are organized. If you have a studio, make sure it is spotless. How messy is your desk? Clean it up and remove all clutter. As professional organizers say, "everything has a place, everything in its place."

The natural formation of the country is the soldier's best ally; but a power of estimating the adversary, of controlling the forces of victory, and of shrewdly calculating difficulties, dangers and distances, constitutes the test of a great general. He who knows these things, and in fighting puts his knowledge into practice, will win his battles. He who knows them not, nor practices them, will surely be defeated.

Learn to use what you have. It's not always about buying more equipment and gadgets to make better photos.

Estimate all things in advance including your scheduling.

Keep a notebook for the details of shoots that you may need to repeat for certain clients to keep consistency, i.e. where you position lights, settings, type of backgrounds, etc.

If fighting is sure to result in victory, then you must fight, even though the ruler forbids it; if fighting will not result in victory, then you must not fight even at the ruler's bidding.

You're the one who calls the shots. If you are really good at what you do, don't let others involved tell you what to do, if you know in the end it will be a mistake. Be strong in your convictions.

The general who advances without coveting fame and retreats without fearing disgrace, whose only thought is to protect his country and do good service for his sovereign, is the jewel of the kingdom.

Be confident and don't second guess yourself. Don't suffer from impostor syndrome. And if you do, don't worry, we all do, from time to time. Always have your client's best interests in mind. And remember to build a reputation of professionalism and excellence.

Regard your soldiers as your children, and they will follow you into the deepest valleys; look upon them as your own beloved sons, and they will stand by you even unto death.

Develop loyalty by taking care of those around you. Make it so that your clients and employees will NEVER leave you. Show genuine interest and caring and spend time working on the details of each and every shot.

Hence the experienced soldier, once in motion, is never bewildered; once he has broken camp, he is never at a loss.

Develop your craft so you minimize mistakes and always have solutions to the problems that come up. Focus on each and every detail of your shoots to make them perfect. Get it right in camera and don't rely on postproduction as a crutch to fix things.

CHAPTER 11: SITUATIONS

When a chieftain is fighting in his own territory, it is dispersive ground.

Home advantage is nice. Aspire to create the perfect studio for your business. Make is comfortable for you and your clients.

When he has penetrated into hostile territory, but to no great distance, it is facile ground.

Don't make it easy to quit. Burn your boats and bridges so you don't have an easy way out.

Ground, the possession of which imports great advantage to either side, for instance a bottle neck, is contentious ground.

Take advantage of good opportunities. If you land a great client, don't take them for granted. Always keep in contact with them so you are always in mind.

On desperate ground, fight. If you fight with all your might, there is a chance of life; whereas death is certain if you cling to your corner.

While you should never allow yourself to get into desperate situations, if you find yourself in one, do whatever it takes to win and get out of that situation. Be persistent and don't accept small setbacks as defeat and a reason to quit. Make your story, the greatest comeback story.

Those who were called skillful leaders of old knew how to drive a wedge between the enemy's front and rear; to prevent co-operation between his large and small divisions; to hinder the good troops from rescuing the bad, the officers from rallying their men.

Divide and conquer. How are you being personally stretched in two different directions? While one can argue with the saying, "He who chases two rabbits catches none," this division can impede progress. What can you eliminate that will help you to become more focused?

When it was to their advantage, they made a forward move; when otherwise, they stopped still.

Don't take action that doesn't benefit you. It may be friends or family asking for free shoots. It may be coming home and watching TV instead of reading a great book like the one you are reading now, wink-wink. Don't be stagnant. Always be growing. Focus on how to grow your business year over year.

If asked how to cope with a great host of the enemy in orderly array and on the point of marching to the attack, I should say: "Begin by seizing something which your opponent holds dear; then he will be amenable to your will."

You will be in a powerful place when you are able to say, "I have what you want." Develop your skills and make offers that are so irresistible to you clients, that they can't say no to you.

Rapidity is the essence of war: take advantage of the enemy's unreadiness, make your way by unexpected routes, and attack unguarded spots.

Execute the ideas that you have quickly. Don't let them just stew and sit there. Take action. I love the quote, "the problem is that you think you have time." The clock is ticking on all of us. There is no tomorrow. Act now, act fast!

Make forays in fertile country in order to supply your army with food.

You should feel obligated to make plenty of money to sustain your business. Don't settle for making just enough to get by. Don't be afraid of success. Your business needs money for it to survive. It needs to grow. Money will provide more marketing campaigns, equipment, more ads, better websites, employees, a nice studio and the list goes on. Make sure you are in a market that has money to spend.

Carefully study the well-being of your men, and do not overtax them. Concentrate your energy and hoard your strength.

How is your health? Are you eating right, are you getting the sleep you need? Are you exercising daily? If not, start today. Start slow. Maybe remove the soda and drink flavored seltzer or just water. Make sure your bedroom is pitch black. Try and not watch TV or stare at your phone right before you go to bed. Take a walk the first thing in the morning. Your body is meant to be moving, not sitting at a desk or on a couch all day and night. A healthier you will make you a better competitor.

Don't overtax your equipment. Flashes can burn out or overheat if you fire them too rapidly.

Keep your army continually on the move and devise unfathomable plans.

You should always be moving forward with your business. Growth should be a primary objective for your business. Create a plan for your photography business that will exceed your wildest dreams!

Throw your soldiers into positions whence there is no escape, and they will prefer death to flight. If they will face death, there is nothing they may not achieve.

Setup your life so that success is the only outcome. This has the tone of burning your boats and bridges so you can't retreat.

But there is some wisdom in having "outs" and backup plans. Don't put all your eggs in one basket comes to mind.

Prohibit the taking of omens and do away with superstitious doubts. Then, until death itself comes, no calamity need be feared.

Think positive. Be the positive one in the group, always inspiring others. Who have you inspired today?

If our soldiers are not overburdened with money, it is not because they have a distaste for riches; if their lives are not unduly long, it is not because they are disinclined to longevity.

It's OK to want money. Businesses need it to survive. People need it to survive. You can do a lot more good in the world with money than you can without it. As the saying goes, "I've been rich, and I've been poor and rich is better." But don't obsess over money. Obsess over creating excellent images and excellent experiences for your clients. The money will come.

A long healthy life is also important. Make your health the number one priority in your life. Cut out the garbage, processed foods that so many of us eat. Exercise the first thing in the morning before you even check your emails. Get it out of the way, even if it is only for 5 minutes.

On the day they are ordered out to battle, your soldiers may weep, those sitting up bedewing their garments, and those lying down letting the tears run down their cheeks.

This isn't because they are cowardly, but because they are ready to fight hard and know they may die. Um, no thanks. Make sure you are happy in your career. Learn to let go of the problem clients, don't take the jobs that you know will make you miserable. Life is way too short to go to a job you hate. And life is certainly too short to go through it struggling financially. For some people it's almost OK to struggle financially as its accepted as a norm. It's not. Set high goals for yourself and do what it takes to reach them.

The skillful tactician may be likened to an aggressive snake. Strike at its head, and you will be attacked by its tail; strike at its tail, and you will be attacked by its head; strike at its middle, and you will be attacked by head and tail both.

Don't be a one trick pony. Always have a counter response to anything that is thrown your way. Do not give up when you are confronted with a no. A good salesperson always has a response when their offer is rejected. Have multiple items to sell your clients.

The principle on which to manage an army is to set up one standard of courage which all must reach.

Just as an entire army must have the same high standards to succeed, all your contact points with your clients should be impressive and up to a high standard. Your email address (no hotmail.com accounts, get your own), your email communications, your website, your business card, your social media pages, your voice mail message, your appearance, your studio, your car, the delivery of your images; each should be impressive on its own. Take lessons from luxury brands. Look at their websites, go to their stores, sign up for their emails. How does the experience feel?

It is the business of a general to be quiet and thus ensure secrecy; upright and just, and thus maintain order. He must be able to mystify his officers and men by false reports and appearances, and thus keep them in total ignorance.

Don't give away your secrets if you have any. While it's nice to be able to brag about certain things, sometimes we should just keep our methods to ourselves.

On open ground, I would keep a vigilant eye on my defenses. On ground of intersecting highways, I would consolidate my alliances.

What alliances can you make within your market? What joint ventures can you create? What businesses can you approach that can refer business to you. There's a retail store near me that sells ballet slippers. I always walk by and think I should approach them and ask if they want to have a picture day for their clients. One that would drive business for them as they could contact their old clients and offer some discounts and a photo opportunity. It's not really my market, but it's an opportunity.

On difficult ground, I would keep pushing on along the road.

Keep pushing yourself forward. Persistence always pays off and is rewarded. Keep on keeping on.

"Nothing in this world can take the place of persistence. Talent will not: nothing is more common than unsuccessful men with talent. Genius will not; unrewarded genius is almost a proverb. Education will not: the world is full of educated derelicts. Persistence and determination alone are omnipotent." – Calvin Coolidge

On desperate ground, I would proclaim to my soldiers the hopelessness of saving their lives. "Burn your baggage and impedimenta, throw away your stores and provisions, choke up the wells, destroy your cooking-stoves, and make it plain to your men that they cannot survive, but must fight to the death." "The only chance of life lies in giving up all hope of it."

This is pretty dismal, but if you are on your last legs, go out with a bang. Have the fire in your belly to succeed.

We cannot enter into alliance with neighboring princes until we are acquainted with their designs. We are not fit to lead an army on the march unless we are familiar with the face of the country—its mountains and forests, its pitfalls and precipices, its marshes and swamps. We shall be unable to turn natural advantages to account unless we make use of local guides.

Be careful with whom you partner with and do your proper due diligence. All agreements should be in writing no matter who you are dealing with. When it comes to money, do not let any amounts owed to you accrue. It's a sure sign you will lose your money.

Bestow rewards without regard to rule, issue orders without regard to previous arrangements; and you will be able to handle a whole army as though you had to do with but a single man.

I reward good clients that are flexible by giving them something extra. I may need to reschedule a shoot on occasion, and I reward clients who don't complain about it with more time, more shots, a discount or free retouch. Often, I won't even mention it, until the end of the shoot, so it's not expected, but then greatly appreciated.

For it is precisely when a force has fallen into harm's way that is capable of striking a blow for victory.

You become strong when your back is pressed to the wall and your options are limited. But it's a horrible place to be. Build your business so this can never happen.

CHAPTER 12: ATTACK BY FIRE

There are five ways of attacking with fire. The first is to burn soldiers in their camp; the second is to burn stores; the third is to burn baggage trains; the fourth is to burn arsenals and magazines; the fifth is to hurl dropping fire amongst the enemy.

This sounds brutal but it should be a reminder that business can be brutal. You may not lose your business to fire, but it may be from another destructive force. Make sure you are insured.

In order to carry out an attack, we must have means available.

If you are just starting out, make sure you have some money to put into your business. You need money for gear, your website, and advertising. If on a tight budget, buy used or budget gear and put all of your money into a slick website and great marketing.

There is a proper season for making attacks with fire, and special days for starting a conflagration.

Your business may be seasonal, weddings for instance. Think about alternative genres in the off season. Can you make any promotions during the seasonal holidays for your business? All photographers can consider a playful advertising campaign with "off-beat holidays" like National Ice Cream Day, celebrated the third Sunday of July. Or how about National Fettuccine Alfredo day in February? Check out https://nationaldaycalendar.com/calendar-at-a-glance/ for some fun ideas.

Unhappy is the fate of one who tries to win his battles and succeed in his attacks without cultivating the spirit of enterprise; for the result is waste of time and general stagnation.

By starting a photography business, you already have the spirit of enterprise. Always be creative and look for ways to promote your business. Work hard to develop relationships with people and organizations that can send you a steady stream of business. If you are opening a studio, try and locate directly next to a business that can give you business. If you want to be a fashion photographer, open a studio office next to a fashion magazine or modeling agency. If you shoot actor headshots, open next to an acting school.

Hence the saying: The enlightened ruler lays his plans well ahead; the good general cultivates his resources.

It has been said already many times, plan your business. What resources or contacts do you have at your disposal now, that you haven't taken advantage of as of yet?

Move not unless you see an advantage; use not your troops unless there is something to be gained; fight not unless the position is critical.

Be efficient. Use software and other tools to automate as many tasks as possible. Consider hiring a virtual assistant to help you. And the best decision I made was to outsource my retouching. I have so much more time because of it.

Hence the enlightened ruler is heedful, and the good general full of caution. This is the way to keep a country at peace and an army intact.

Don't make risky decisions. While I can't image how it could possibly happen even once, every year people die by getting hit by a train while doing a photoshoot on the tracks. People also fall off of cliffs to get close to the edge for a photo.

Make sure you back up your photos. Use dual card slots whenever possible. Back up your website. Take care with how you handle your memory cards and hard drives.

Chapter 13: THE USE OF SPIES

Raising a host of a hundred thousand men and marching them great distances entails heavy loss on the people and a drain on the resources of the State. The daily expenditure will amount to a thousand ounces of silver. Thus, what enables the wise sovereign and the good general to strike and conquer, and achieve things beyond the reach of ordinary men, is foreknowledge, information coming from spies.

Running a business can be expensive and can wear you down. Make sure you have all the knowledge possible to gain any and all advantages. If you have corporate clients, do you know anyone that works there that can give you helpful "inside" information?

Do you have any clients or know of anyone that worked with one of your competitors? What information can you ask to help you in your business?

Without subtle ingenuity of mind, one cannot make certain of the truth of their reports.

Do your best to validate any rumors you may hear.
From your perspective, always speak the truth.

Whether the object be to crush an army, to storm a city, or to assassinate an individual, it is always necessary to begin by finding out the names of the attendants, the aides-de- camp, and doorkeepers and sentries of the general in command. Our spies must be commissioned to ascertain these.

We can certainly question the moral use of spies in our business and I don't think you should assassinate any of your competitors, but it can't hurt to ask questions of those that have knowledge that you can benefit from.

Remember and use people's names. Use the name of your client often during a session or meeting as it will make them feel more comfortable.

The end and aim of spying in all its varieties is knowledge of the enemy; and this knowledge can only be derived, in the first instance, from the converted spy.

You can also do your own spying as well to gain knowledge of your competitors. Check out their websites, sign up to their newsletters, make enquires as to their offerings so to get a better understanding of their services.

Conversely, there are also those who operate their businesses without even the thought of what their competitors are up to. They have their own vision and plans and spend all of their time bringing their vision to life. They don't have the time or the concern to care about what their competitors are doing. For these people, "the game" is only being played with themselves. I personally don't agree. While I don't spy, I do want to know what my competitors are charging and what their offers include. Just like in real estate, you need to know your "comps" to know what a property is worth.

Where do you stand?

CONCLUSION

Take your business seriously. It is really up to you to decide how successful you want your business to be. While a lot of the ideas may sound like simple and obvious platitudes, just one idea implemented, can make a great impact on your business and on your life.

Don't accept mediocrity from your images, your business, your marketing, or your life. There are enough resources out there for you to take advantage of to make your business a smashing success. As long as you have the will and the determination to be the best, you will succeed. It just takes work. **PUT IN THE WORK!**

Workbook Section

Below are the questions asked throughout the book for you to fill in.

What would be the best way for you to start your day?

What can you do to cultivate client loyalty?

Think of one new shoot you can do next week that can stretch your creativity a bit.

Do you have any guarantees? What is your procedure for dissatisfied clients?

What do you need to work on in general?

Can you think of any friction points that exist with you or your business in relation to your clients or team?

If you have your own studio location, what can you do to improve it?

How fit and energetic are you? What will you change today to have more energy?

What new technique do you wish to learn that will help you with your business?

What online course or workshop can you take that you can benefit from?

Using the law of reciprocity, what offer can you give in order to get more business?

What is the plan for your business? What are your monthly profit goals? What will you have to do in order to achieve them?

List your competitors and reach out to them for some potential collaboration. Make sure your work is on par with them.

In what areas are your clients resisting you? Is it your prices, quality, turnaround, location?

What are the things in your business that you know you should do, even though you don't want to do them?

Do you have any large projects that you have been avoiding that you can take action on this week?

Are there other potential markets can you market to?

How can you bring innovation to your business?

How hard did you fight for your business today?

How are you positioning your business; as a low-end volume shop or a high-end boutique?

What part of your business is stressing you out and what can you do to eliminate that stress?

How will your business become the best in your market?

Are you chasing too many rabbits? What makes you the most profit? What makes the least profit? Where should you focus?

What new project are you thinking about, but are not acting on? How can you get it done this month?

What is your plan for growth?

Who have you inspired today? Make it a daily goal to do so.

Every touch point of your business should be a fantastic experience for your clients. What can you do to improve each touchpoint? (Email, voicemail message, business card, website, social media, studio, clothing, deliverables, car, etc.)

Is your business insured? Look for a liability policy with errors and omissions as well as theft and damage.

How do you backup your photos?

Are you committed to make your photography business a success?

About the Author

Bradley Lau lives in Manhattan and makes a living as a corporate headshot photographer. He is completely self-taught. He started in 2003 and has explored most genres of photography. When he is not shooting headshots, he works on a number of side projects including writing books, officiating weddings, and building websites. Like many entrepreneurs, he is always working on a new project. His current project is the website www.shootforthemoney.com/

www.ingramcontent.com/pod-product-compliance
Lightning Source LLC
Chambersburg PA
CBHW051538240526
45465CB00027B/714